WAYNE'S WORLD

EXTREME CLOSE-UP

WAYNE'S WORLD

EXTREME CLOSE-UP

By Mike Myers and Robin Ruzan
Photographs by Norman Ng

●

CADER BOOKS

●

HYPERION
NEW YORK

The Excellent Cast
Garth Algar courtesy of Dana Carvey

Models: Jim Biederman, Marci Klein,
Christine Lauria, Erin Maroney,
Donna Perillo, Jim Pitt, Sandy Restrepo,
Mike Shoemaker
Hair: Kathrine Gordon
Makeup: Courtney Corell
Props: Danny Bleier
Roadie: Speedy Rosenthal
Costumes: Ed Falco
Art Director: Edie Baskin

Special thanks to
Eric Gardner, Greg Greenberg
and Christopher Ward.

Produced by
Cader Books
24 W. 10 Street
New York, N.Y. 10011

Cover and Book Design: Charles Kreloff
Production: Lee Goodman & Judi Orlick
Photo research: Elsa Peterson

Photo Credits
p. 12: Europress/Globe Photos, Everett Collection
p. 13: Gabor Rona/Everett Collection
p. 22: Photofest
p. 29: Bob V. Noble/Globe Photos,
© George F. Thompson, 1979/Globe Photos, Richard
Open/Globe Photos, John Barrett/Globe Photos
p. 31: Everett Collection
p. 45: Merlino/Shooting Star, Giraudon/Art Resource,
© J. Donoso/Sygma
p. 55: © Jack Swenson/Tom Stack and Associates
p. 57: © Tony Freeman/PhotoEdit
(2), © Joel Gordon 1985
pp. 58 - 59: Everett Collection, © 1990 Stephen
Harvey/LGI, Everett Collection; Photofest
p. 66: © Gary Walts/The Image Works
p. 70: Suzanne Tenner/courtesy of Paramount
Pictures Corp.
p. 86: © John Atashian/Retna, © Adam Scull/Globe
Photos, Everett Collection
p. 92: Everett Collection

Library of Congress Cataloging-in-Publication Data
Myers, Mike.
    Wayne's World: extreme close-up / Wayne Campbell as
told to Mike Myers and Robin Ruzan. – 1st Ed.
        p. cm.
    ISBN 1-56282-979-3 : $7.95
    1. Saturday Night Live (Television program)
2. Campbell, Wayne (Fictitious character) 3. American wit
and humor. I. Ruzan, Robin. II. Title.
PN1992. 77.S273M94 1991
791. 45'72–dc20   91-41285
                                                              CIP

First edition
10 9 8 7 6 5 4 3 2 1

DEDICATION

Mike would like to dedicate this book to
Robin, Bunny, Eric, Peter, Paul, Linda,
Irving and Jordan.

Robin would like to dedicate this book to
Mike, Linda, Irving, Jordan, Bunny, Eric,
Peter and Paul.

CONTENTS

FOREWORD

When they called me up and asked me to write a book I said "no way" and they said "way" and I said "no-oo wa-ay" and they said "way" and I said "noooooo waaaaaay" and they said "way" and then I got call-waiting and I asked them to hang on a second. Then I pressed down the receiver and said "Hello" and it was Garth and he said "Hey, Wayne, what's up" and I said "Garth, I can't talk, I'm on the other line with these publishing guys and they want me to write a book" and Garth said "no way" and I said "way" and he said "no-oo wa-ay" and I said "way" and he said "noooooo waaaaaay" and I said "way." Then I said, "Hey, man, I'm going to have to call you back" and Garth said "Cool" and then I pressed down the receiver and said "Hello" and they said "Hi" and I said "I'm sorry, where were we" and they said "Way" and I said "Oh, yeah, no way" and they said "Way" and I said "What kind of format do you want me to do?" and they said "Something like *Wayne's World: A to Z*" and I said "No way" and they said "Way" and I . . . Well, you get the idea. Anyway, so here's my book.

GO TO PAGE 33 FOR A CASH PRIZE... NOW!

TOP TEN ALBUMS

TOP TEN ALBUMS PARTY TIME EXCELLENT

10. Meatloaf, *Bat Out of Hell*

9. Sweet, *Desolation Blvd*

8. Alice Cooper, *Hey Stoopid*

7. Aerosmith, *Toys in the Attic*

6. Nana Mouskouri, *Love Songs Greek Style: The Best of Nana Mouskouri* (Nana Mouskouri is the Greek chanteuse who has sold millions of records in Europe. I included her as a sorbet, to clear the palate.)

5. Led Zeppelin, *Houses of the Holy*

4. Led Zeppelin, *Physical Graffiti*

3. Led Zeppelin, the one with an old man carrying a bundle of sticks on his back.

2. Led Zeppelin boxed set

1. Aerosmith, *Pump*

TOP TEN BABES OF ALL TIME

TOP TEN   PARTY TIME
BABES OF ALL TIME   EXCELLENT

10. **Julia Roberts**. Major lippage.
 9. **Elle McPherson**. She's a McBabe. She's a McFox. McSchwing!!
 8. **Josephine Baker**. Remember I said of *all time*. Josephine Baker was a babe in the '20s who, although the victim of the prevailing racial mores of her native United States, became the toast of Paris, known primarily for her exotic Banana Dance.
 7. **Betty Rubble**, from *The Flintstones*. Even though she's a cartoon, she's still a fox. Bam Bam.
 6. **Farrah Fawcett**. She redefined hairstyles for an entire generation of mall chicks.
 5. **Irene Ryan** who played Granny on *The Beverly Hillbillies*. I put her in here as a sorbet, to clear the palate once again.

4. Heather Locklear. Rrrregglle. Major Schwing action.

3. Garth's mom. I'm sorry, I know she's his mom but she's a babe. Schwing!!

2. Kim Basinger. "When I think about Kim Basinger I touch myself. When I think about Kim Basinger I touch myself."

1. Madonna. She's the Queen of Babe-elonia. Her babe-a-tude is cruel and unusual and I believe there is legislation pending to curb such dangerous levels of babeosity. She's magically babetitious. I should know. I'm a licensed babe-tician. She'd give a dog a bone. And the beauty of it is, I've had her. Way!!

TOP TEN WORST BABES OF ALL TIME

10. Madame, the puppet creation by the late Waylon Flowers

9. Cruella, from *101 Dalmatians*

8. Nurse Ratched

7. Mrs. Howell from *Gilligan's Island*

6. The Countess de St. Germaine (1720 -1762)

5. My vice principal in junior high (trust me)

4. Leona Helmsley (She even makes us doctors squeamish.)

3. Babe Ruth (I'm sorry, he just doesn't turn me on.)

2. Milton Berle when he would dress like a woman (And they called him Uncle Miltie?)

1. Any bearded lady of any given circus

BABE TALK

You know, a lot of times Garth and I will talk about babes (who doesn't). Sometimes we get very competitive and try to outdo each other.

Here are some tips on how to talk babe. One helpful hint is to go back through old textbooks, looking for amazing suffixes or prefixes. For example, some amazing suffixes are -ation; -osity; -ness and some amazing prefixes are mega-, robo-, multi-, etc.

Anyway, here's a typical conversation Garth and I might have upon seeing a babe.

WAYNE: She's a babe.

GARTH: She's a mega-babe.

WAYNE: In terms of babeness, it's no quarter asked and no quarter given.

GARTH: She's a babe-aholic and she needs help.

WAYNE: She's from Babe-alon. She's Babe-alonian.

GARTH: She's babetitious.

I should know, I'm a licensed babe-tician.

WAYNE: If she were president she would be Baberaham Lincoln.

GARTH: In Latin she's known as *babia majora.*

WAYNE: Her babocity is diabolical. Way to go. Good work my friend.

WAYNE and **GARTH:** Owwwwww!

BEEV'S AD

Okay, so you know Garth's Dad, Beev, right? Anyway I promised him I would let him run an ad in my book so here it is – Beev's Ad:

MAIN STREET

MAPLE STREET

TOP TEN THINGS BEEV SAYS

10. Hey you kids, buy something or leave.

9. Are you gonna buy that magazine? This isn't a library.

8. Either you empty out your pockets or you are banned from the store.

7. Shouldn't you kids be in class?

6. Eat your junk food outside of the store.

5. Are you gonna buy that magazine? This isn't a library.

4. Wayne's the coolest guy in the world.

3. All the chicks dig Wayne big time.

2. I wish I could be as cool as Wayne.

1. Hi, my name is Beev. I'm a big sphincter.

CABLE ACCESS AROUND THE WORLD

ANGUS'S WORLD

"I think I'm going to blow haggis!"

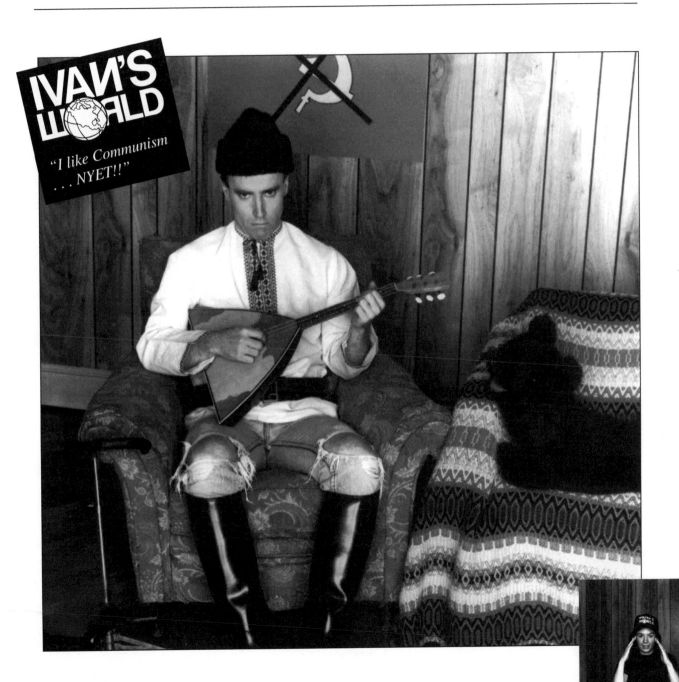

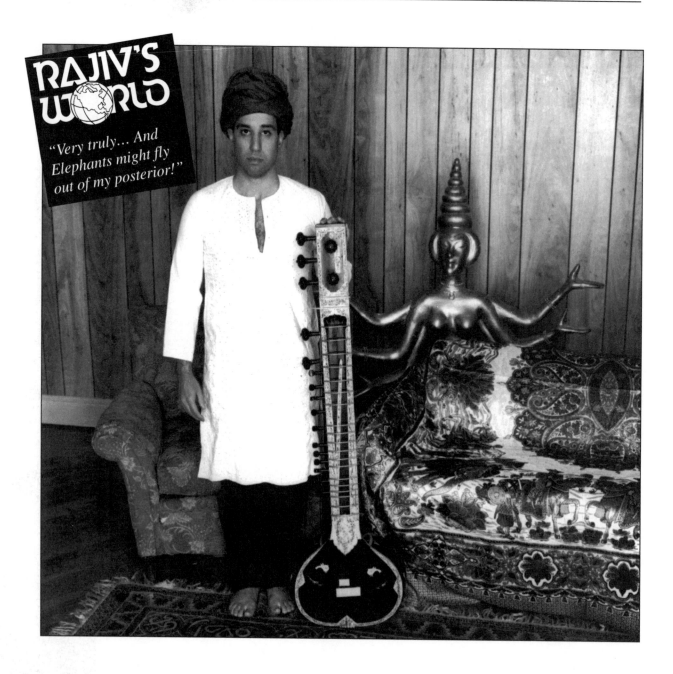

RAJIV'S WORLD

"Very truly... And Elephants might fly out of my posterior!"

WONG'S WORLD

"The Peking Circus is in my breakfast nook where I eat my Dim Sum every morning."

CAHIERS DU CINÉMA: WAYNE'S FILM LIBRARY

BEST *STUFF ABOUT MOVIES* *PARTY TIME*
WORST *FOR ALL TIME* *EXCELLENT*

Okay, so now I'd like to do my list of Best/Worst Stuff About Movies.

BEST MOVIE OF ALL TIME: *The Graduate*. Katherine Ross, what a babe! Rrrregglle!

WORST MOVIE OF ALL TIME: *Ice Castles*, starring Holly something. It's a chick movie. Not only is it a chick movie, it's a bad chick movie. It's worse than *The Bear*. It sucked donkey.

BEST ACADEMY-AWARD WINNING ACTOR WHO WON AND THEN DISAPPEARED: F. Murray Abraham. He was brilliant in *Amadeus* and then poof! Houdini. Did you know he played a grape in a Fruit of the Loom commercial?

WORST FOREIGN FILM: *Der Tangospieler*. One of the last films produced under the old East German regime, *Der Tangospieler*, or *The Tango Player*, is a well-crafted ironic picture dealing with injustice in the police state. Although it brilliantly satirizes the excesses of dialectical materialism, I found it stilted and politically naive.

THE MOST HANDSOME GUY IN THE MOVIES EVER: French actor Gerard Depardieu…Not!!

He looks like something I ate and dropped.

JUST DIDN'T GET IT AWARD: This is an honorary award given to those films that, I'm sorry, I just didn't get. The first movie is *Big*, starring Tom Hanks. Now I love Tom Hanks and this film captures childhood with the same loving detail that François Truffaut's *The Four Hundred Blows* did. Having said that, I think the film had major problems.

Early on in the movie we see our hero, a young boy, at a carnival, humiliated in front of his girlfriend because he's not big enough to get on this ride. It was brilliantly played. Very touching. I thought to myself, "How many times has this happened to me? Man this is going to be a great film." Then he puts a coin into this Fortune Telling machine that's not even plugged in, makes a wish and before you know it: He's Tom Hanks. A fully grown man. Shyeah Righttt!! That might happen . . . And monkeys might fly out of my butt! What the hell is that? I mean that's so unbelievable. You had a perfectly good movie about childhood and then ka-boom, out of the blue, they make him this fully grown man. What did they do, make two movies and fuse them together? Did they think we wouldn't notice? What's that all about? Good movie, very believable . . . NOT!!

Okay, the next movie is *Field of Dreams*, a movie about this man trying to make his farm survive in the 1980s. For like the first twenty minutes I thought, "Man, this is going to be our generation's *Grapes of Wrath*, truly." But the next thing you know, he's hearing voices and playing baseball with dead people.

What the hell is that? That would never happen. It's pail. It's bucket. I've never heard voices and I've certainly never played any sport with dead people. Dead people are dead. It just doesn't happen.

Two movies with promise, destroyed by stuff that's just completely unbelievable. Is it just me?

BEST BABE IN A MAJOR MOTION PICTURE: Heather Locklear in *The Swamp Thing*. Bad movie, great snoobs.

RUNNER UP: Adrienne Barbeau in . . . a whole bunch of movies.

BEST ADULT FILM: It's a tossup between *Field of Reems* starring Seka and *Bright Lights, Big Titties* starring Tory Wells.

BEST SUPPORTING ACTOR IN A FILM: Joe Pesci in *Goodfellas*. I didn't see the movie but I love his name. It's like "I'm feeling a bit Pesci, you know, like I could or could not eat fish. I'm just Pesci."

TOP TEN THINGS THAT MAKE YOU BLOW CHUNKS

Don't underestimate the necessity of holding back a hurl. If you hurl and someone catches a whiff of it they are going to spew. And if you blow chunks chances are someone else is going to honk, setting off a reverse peristaltic chain reaction.

Therefore try to avoid the following:

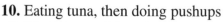

WAYNE'S WORLD TOP TEN PARTY TIME EXCELLENT

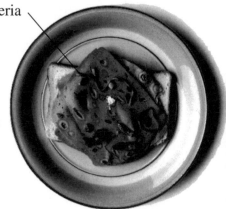

10. Eating tuna, then doing pushups

9. The Mystery Meat they serve at the cafeteria

8. Watching someone else blow chunks

7. Having a big fat guy pop his pimples on you

6. Having a bump on your face that turns out to be a nest of baby spiders

5. The safety films they show in metal shop

4. Disco music

3. Man's inhumanity to man

2. Eating the Mystery Meat and then doing pushups

1. Beev, because he's such a big sphincter

CRISIS MANAGEMENT: AFFIRMATIONS

Although I'm incredibly cool, sometimes
I lose sight of the beauty and splendor that dwells
deep within my soul. So to remind myself I recite an
affirmation (a strong, positive statement) every day.
Here are some words of inspiration to help you tap into
your own spiritual powers.

Repeat them over and over to yourself on a daily basis.

I AM NOT A GIMP.

HEATHER LOCKLEAR DIGS ME BIG TIME.

I AM NOT A TOOL.

I THINK SHE LIKES ME . . . (Omit the NOT!!!)

MONKEYS MIGHT FLY OUT OF MY BUTT IF I BELIEVE
AND VISUALIZE THEM TO DO SO.

I THINK I'M GOING TO HURL SO THERE MUST BE A
LESSON I NEED TO LEARN.

I WISH I WERE MORE LIKE WAYNE.

LOOK AT THE UNIT ON <u>ME</u>!

I <u>AM</u> WORTHY, I <u>AM</u> WORTHY!

*Look at the
unit on <u>me</u>!*

MEET DR. WAYNE

I'm not a doctor, but I play one on TV.

Okay, so I don't play one on TV, but if I did I'd want to specialize in the study of so-called "minor" temporary, nonfatal conditions that continue to go unrecognized and untreated.

Sure my colleagues at the Royal Academy might scoff at my seemingly trivial medical pursuit, but they are merely curs nipping at the heels of genius.

Below is a compilation of a life's work dedicated to lesser-known ailments that are no less important:

Bed Head
The condition by which your hair takes the shape of the position your head was on the pillow while you were sleeping.

Amnesia Frigedotis
Going to get something out of the refrigerator and then just standing there with the door open, forgetting what you wanted.

Eye Spasm
Low-grade muscle spasm (especially the ones you get in your eye) that you think makes you look really weird but is actually not visible to anyone.

Swamp Mouth
A bad taste in your mouth. It sometimes tastes like gasoline. It's impervious to tooth brushing, mouthwash and a whole pack of gum.

Somnoped
Foot's asleep.

Concert Ring
Ringing in your
ears after a concert.

The Manilow Complex
A tune that you hear first thing when you get
up and can't get out of your head. You try
putting on your favorite album to drown it
out. For example, you unfortunately hear
"Mandy" by Barry Manilow first thing in the
morning. Later on in the day, you put on an
Aerosmith tune to get rid of "Mandy." You
think it's going to work but instead you find
yourself humming in your mind, "Love in an
elevator . . . And I need you today, Oh,
Mandy." Brutal!

Hat Head
The condition by
which your hair
takes the shape of
your hat.

Halls/Minute Maid Syndrome
Having a cough drop and then drinking
orange juice.

Wayne's Complaint
Stomachache after being
kicked in the balls.

**Fromage Digititus or Cheese
Popcorn Hands**
The condition that occurs after excessive eating of cheese popcorn. Its symptoms are an
orange discoloration of the fingers (or digits)
that will defy even the harshest and most
abrasive cleansers.

Ur-ine trouble
Aromatic asparagus
pee or pee that
smells like Sugar
Smacks even
though you haven't
had Sugar Smacks.

HOW TO DO A DREAM SEQUENCE

You know, a lot of people ask me, "How is it that you and Garth get in and out of dream sequences on your show when the budget is so low?"

Well, what we do is use our hands to simulate the ripple dissolve or flexatron effect that your more high-budgeted television shows use.

Here is a diagram showing how you can achieve this effect. We can't tell you what to put in your dreams, we can only instruct you on how to get in and out of them safely.

1   **2**   **3**

By the way, the phrase is spelled: Diddle liddle la, Diddle liddle la. It's pronounced "did´-el lid´-el la," repeated very quickly over and over again. (See Flip Book, p. 35)

EMERSON LAKE AND ?

Emerson Lake and Zadora

Emerson Lake and Arnold Palmer

Emerson Lake and Thatcher

Emerson Lake and Ricki Lake

Emerson Lake and Campbell

Emerson Lake and Algar

YOU AND THE ENVIRONMENT– HELP SAVE THE PLANET

RECYCLE YOUR HURL. When I have a hurl on deck, I grab some sort of receptacle. Most chunkage is rich in nutrients and can make an excellent fertilizer.

TOP TEN FEMALE CARTOON CHARACTERS WE'D ALL LIKE TO HAVE SEX WITH

10. **Judy Jetson**

9. **Jane Jetson**

8. **Josie and all the Pussycats**

7. **Veronica**

6. **Betty**

5. **The cat** that leaned against wet paint, causing Pépé le Pew to think she was a skunk.

4. **Bugs Bunny** when he would put on a dress and pretend to be a girl bunny.

3. **Sassy**, Dino's love interest on *The Flintstones*.

2. **Jessica Rabbit**

1. **Betty Rubble**

SHAMELESS FILLER

We had to come up with ninety-six pages because books are printed in increments of thirty-two. It's all part of the binding process. It's very interesting. (See page 56) We were a little short, so I hope you find the following information helpful.

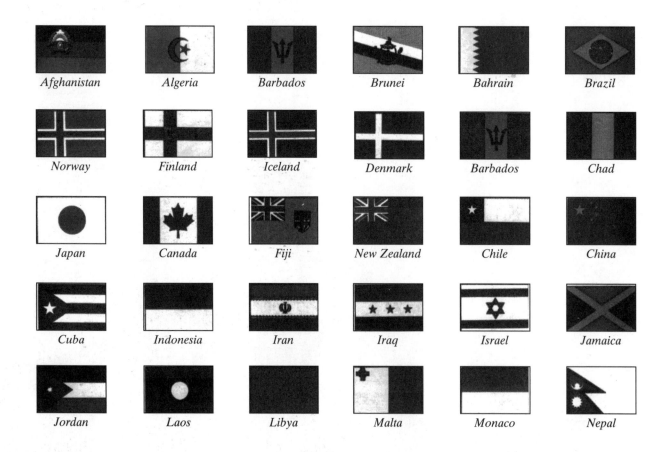

Afghanistan   Algeria   Barbados   Brunei   Bahrain   Brazil

Norway   Finland   Iceland   Denmark   Barbados   Chad

Japan   Canada   Fiji   New Zealand   Chile   China

Cuba   Indonesia   Iran   Iraq   Israel   Jamaica

Jordan   Laos   Libya   Malta   Monaco   Nepal

FISHED IN!

Fished in! Sign of the
fish! Get the net!
Fished you right in!
Caught'm, cleaned'm
and fried'm right up!
Fished you right in.
Wayne the
Bassmaster!

HOW TO DO FISHED IN! AT HOME

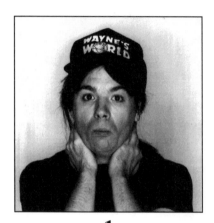

1

2

3

4

5

FLIP BOOK

Hey, wait a minute. What's this rooster doing at the bottom of the page? ⎯⎯⎯⎯

Well, it's to call your attention to the fact that this book is not only a great piece of literature . . . why it's a flip book, too.

Here's how the flip book works.

It creates the illusion of movement through the phenomenon known as persistence of vision. Persistence of vision occurs because there is a lag time between an image being received on the retina and the optical nerve sending that image to the brain. Images are burned into the retina, similar to how if you point a video camera at a light and move it away fast there is a streak, or afterimage, that remains. If you have twenty-four images per second (or frames) as in motion pictures, for example, you create the illusion of movement.

Simply put your thumb on the edge of the book and flip through the pages very quickly. It's that easy.

READING THIS BOOK IS ALL A DREAM . . . OR IS IT????
WHAAAAAA!!!!!!

GARTH

*Here's my best friend,
Garth Algar.*

As you may or may not know, Garth is my best bud and most excellent co-host. We've lived across the street from each other all our lives. Garth's house is a Mock Tudor and I must say—Garth's house smells great. You know how some people's houses have that awful smell— like beef vegetable soup mix and you know they haven't had beef vegetable soup in years. But Garth's house doesn't suffer from Soup Whiff. Instead it's a tasteful melange of pine and potpourri.

I believe that's the handiwork of Garth's mom, Mrs. Hilary Algar. Rrrregglle! What a fox! I'm serious, she's such a fox she should be on the Fox Network. In France she would be known as La Renarde—The Fox. In England she would be hunted by the aristocracy with only her cunning to protect her.

I'm sorry, Garth's got a babe for a mom. He's such a lucky duck. The only thing is she's married to Beev right?

Let's take a look shall we.

Here's a picture of Mrs. Algar and here's a picture of Beev.

The man's a dweeb. How can a dweeb like him be married to a fox like her? It isn't natural. Does this foretell the coming of the Apocalypse? Will tigers lie with antelopes? Will the sky fall? Will there be a rain of toads? Will good prophets turn evil and lead the faithful astray? Will Aaron Neville get that mole removed from his eyebrow? (After that hit with Linda Ronstadt, he surely has the money.)

Mrs. Algar

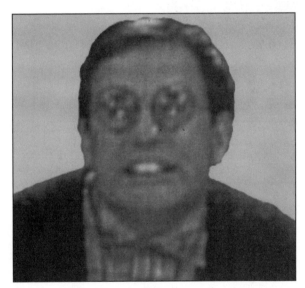

Beev

A GIMP FIGHT

Like every good friendship, there are times when Garth and I fight. Perhaps fight is too strong of a word. It's more like we spar. (See *Spartacus*: Not the chapter—the movie. There's this great scene where they all claim to be Spartacus. That happened to me once when Garth and I were whipping snowballs at cars and we took off, only Garth dropped his notebook with his name written on it. The next day a policeman came to our school and said, "Which one of you is Garth Algar?" and one by one each student stood up and went, "I'm Garth Algar." But when they got to Garth he stood up and said, "I'm Spartacus.")

But I digress.

Our favorite thing to call each other is a gimp which is really handy if you want to get at someone. Done right it's most effective.

Here is a sample gimp fight progression, to try at your leisure.

You're a Gimp.

You're Majorly Gimpish.

You're a Gimpathon.

You're a Gimperama.

You're Gimpoid.

You're Gimptition.

You're Gimptitious.

You're Gimpesque.

You're In-the-style-of-the-gimp.

You're Gimplike.

You have Simulated Gimp-look.

You're Gimp-ed.

You're Begimped.

You're just Gimpy.

When you've run out of gimp stuff, you should admit it, and say "Buds?"

GLOSSARY OF TERMS

WORD	MEANING
Excellent!	Remarkably good.
Party time, Excellent!	Occasion for celebration. Remarkably good.
Not!	Used at the end of a statement of fact, expressing denial, negation or refusal. (Similar to how a negative symbol at the beginning of a mathematical subset renders that subset negative regardless of any possible positive integer within said subset.)
Extreme Close-up!	Drastic camera angle.
You're pail. You're bucket.	You are bad. You are awful.
I'm not worthy!!	I am not deserving!!
Ka-boom!	Resounding explosion.
Take a pill!	Unwind, luxuriate.
Good work, my friend.	You should be lauded for your labor.
Unnecessary Zoom!	Superfluous camera angle.
Silent Scream!	Voiceless bellow.
Schwing!!	My word she is attractive!
He Shoots! He Scores!	He is victorious. He is successful.
Shyeeeeaahh! RRiiiggghhhtt!	Certainly! Of, course!
Party On Wayne! Party On Garth!	Celebrate, Wayne! Celebrate, Garth!
I think I'm gonna hurl!!	I believe the possibility exists for me to vomit.
And monkeys might fly out of my butt!	The chances of something like that happening are less than if primates were to soar from my backside!
Aurora Rocks!	Aurora is indeed a lively city.
It sucked.	I must admit, it was not very good.
A chick movie	A film geared towards a predominantly female audience.
Rrrregglle!	An onomatopoeic utterance pioneered by Jerry the Dentist on TV's *The Dick Van Dyke Show*.

HOW TO PLAY ELECTRIC GUITAR WAYNE'S WAY

Shown here is the correct way to hold the plectrum (or pick), except that most people don't hold their pick like this so ignore it.

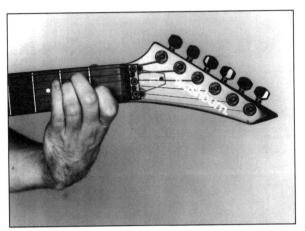

This is an E chord.

I don't know what chord this is, but it should be played fast and loud.

Position A–Run the pick along the length of the strings.(Note: make guitar sounds with mouth to supplement the effect.)

Position B–Finishing position. (Note cool face.)

TOP TEN ROCK 'N' ROLL GUYS WHO COULD PASS FOR CHICKS

TOP TEN WAYNE'S WORLD PARTY TIME EXCELLENT

10. The guy from Nelson

9. Sebastian Bach, the lead singer from Skid Row

8. David Bowie (No guff!)

7. The lead singer from The Cult

6. The bass player from Poison

5. The lead singer from Mr. Big

4. The bassist from Warrant

3. Jon Bon Jovi

2. Grace Jones

1. The other guy from Nelson

HEAVY METAL

As I see it, Heavy Metal can be defined as the following: wailing guitar chords and a guy behind the drum kit going mental (with the parameters being speed and loudness, emphasis on the latter).

The only thing about Heavy Metal that I can't get into is devil junk. I'm sorry, devil junk scares me. The Devil probably has amazing clothes but I wouldn't want to party with him.

But whatever kind of metal you're into, whether it be Speed Metal, Thrash Metal, Glam Metal or Pop Metal, you must maintain a certain lifestyle.

Below are some important "Do's" and "Don'ts" of a Heavily Metallic lifestyle:

CATEGORY	BOGUS CHOICE	HEAVILY METALLIC ALTERNATIVE
CAR	Volvo, BMW, Mercedes-Benz	Four-Wheel Monster Vehicle, an Army Jeep as long as it has tunes, or The Bus.
FOODS	Pasta	Kraft Macaroni and Cheese with wieners cut into them. (See Recipe, page 67)
SPORTS	Tennis or Golf	Tractor Pull, Wrestling, or Shot Put.
LITERATURE	Shakespeare (He tapped the collective unconscious, there's no doubt about it, but let's face it— the man can't wail.)	Anything by Ayn Rand and the late Dr. Seuss. *Hop on Pop* would have made a kick-ass metal tune.

HISTORY OF HEAVY METAL

AMOEBA

PROTOZOA

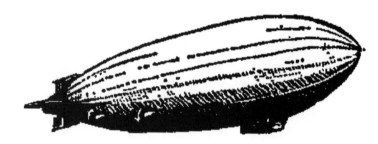

ZEP

HEROES

TOP TEN HEROES   PARTY TIME   EXCELLENT

	HERO	WHY
10.	Robert Plant	The vocal on "Heartbreaker" alone
9.	Mother Teresa	For her altruism
8.	Mel Blanc	Voice of Bugs Bunny (enough said)
7.	Moses	Because
6.	Stan Mikita	Number 21 on the Chicago Blackhawks. He should get a two-minute penalty for looking so good.
5.	Steven Tyler	We're not worthy. (See Transcript, page 74)
4.	Claudia Schiffer	(See Schwing!!)
3.	Fred Flintstone	He's a true Hanna-Barberrian
2.	Thomas Paine	Author of *Rights of Man*, a treatise on the role of the individual within the nation state.
1.	Wayne Gretzky	The god who walked as man, the husband of Janet Jones–good work my friend.

TOP TEN TERMS USED IN HOCKEY THAT SOUND DIRTY

TOP TEN HOCKEY TERMS PARTY TIME EXCELLENT

10. On top of the crease

9. Spearing

8. High sticking

7. Penalty box

6. Power play

5. Dump and chase

4. Wrap around goal

3. Slipped it between the pads

2. Putting your hands on a girl's breast

1. Puck

FAVORITE HOLIDAY

I was going to say that Thanksgiving is my favorite holiday but then I remembered that I always eat too much turkey and it makes me sleepy. You see turkey contains tryptophan which is an amino acid that triggers the sleep mechanism in the brain. This same amino acid can also be found in bananas and until recently was used therapeutically in the treatment of sleep disorders.

But I digress.

Basically what happens is that everyone gets a wicked Turkey Coma. Last year on Thanksgiving I got Turkey Comatose. It was dire. It was diabolical. It was putrid. Also, I don't know about you but stuffing makes me cut. Major "pull my finger" action. It's punitive. It's caustic. It's cruel and unusual. Public safety becomes a priority. You become an abhorrent military option. If you're sick, go see a doctor my friend.

But I digress again.

So, to make a long story short my favorite holiday is Halloween. Last year I went as the Evil

Wayne Campbell. You can tell I'm the Evil Wayne cause I'm wearing a beard. You know like on Star Trek, when they want to make Spock the Evil Spock and all they do is whip a goatee on him.

But the thing I like most about Halloween is that babes always wear costumes that make them look really excellent. So I've compiled a list of the Top Ten Excellent Babe Costumes.

WAYNE'S TOP TEN WORLD

10. **A cat**. Rrrregglle. Form-fitting cat suits. Meowww.
9. **A nurse**. Rrrregglle. Call Randy Mantooth. Rampart, I need help.
8. **A brick**. In that case I'd go as a brick layer.
7. **Pebbles Flintstone**–Bam Bam.
6. **An Indian girl**. Da da da da da da bum bum bum bum bum bum.
5. **A baseball player**. There's something about when a girl dresses like a baseball player because in her attempt at masculinity that which is woman is underscored.
4. **Private school girl**. Those plaid skirts. Oww. Except if she tries to do a little girl voice she should be resoundly slapped.
3. **French maid**–Mais oui.
2. **Playboy bunny**–I am thanking you.
1. **Heather Locklear**. She's magically delicious. She'd give a dog a bone.

Nurse   *Private school girl*

EXCELLENT

PARTY TIME

BABE COSTUMES

EXCELLENT

Indian girl   *Baseball player*   *Pebbles Flintstone*   *French maid*

VITAL INFORMATION

FULL NAME...WAYNE NIBBLET CAMPBELL

SEX ....Yes, please. (AUTHOR'S NOTE: Wayne was the first person to ever put this on a form . . . honest to God.)

BIRTHDAY...September 31st

SUN SIGN ....Leo. Born Libra but prefers Leo because they're good leaders, fiercely loyal, steadfastly honest and moody.

BIRTHPLACE ....In the area of my mother's undercarriage

CURRENT RESIDENCE ....Aurora, Illinois (Suburb 38 miles west of Chicago)

OCCUPATION...Host of a cable access show – Cable 10, Friday nights at 10:30

LISTED OCCUPATION ON PASSPORT ...International Man of Mystery

PARENTS ....One Mother and one Father

MOTHER'S MAIDEN NAME ....Nibblet

HEIGHT...4 ft. 20 inches

WEIGHT..8 stone

EYES...Hazel

HAIR..Shoulder length

HAT..Wayne's World Logo

GLOVE ....7 (hockey)

PERFECT DATE ....February 22nd

PETS ....Dog named Nibblet, Cat named Mr. Nibblet, Trouser snake named Master Nibblet

RELIGION...Nibbletology

CURRENTLY READING ....This book

HOBBIES...The guitar, volcanology, and working the word "nibblet" into this feature

FAVORITE COLOR ....Nibblet Yellow

MOST EMBARRASSING MOMENT ....The time at school when Master Nibblet got caught in my zipper

JCROSSWORD

ACROSS

1. He _____s, he scores!
5. Tape format
8. The best way to eat corn
9. Uma Thurman's initials
10. In Latin a babe would be called a *babia* _____
12. Opposite of No way!
13. Actor Robert _____from TV's *Quincy*
14. Ancient Chinese unit of distance, huh?
15. *Au* _____. What a French fox or "Renarde" says when she dumps you.
16. Hitchcock film: *North by ___*. (abbrev.)
18. See 16 across.
19. Excellent co-host
21. Home state of R.E.M. (abbrev.).
23. Baseball player Ruth or what Heather Locklear is
26. Something disgusting (adj.) Sounds kind of like highness.
27. Ultimate goal in football

DOWN

1. Usual reaction when you see a babe
2. Prostitute
3. Babe doctor
4. Illinois for example
6. The act of throwing up or Celtic sport
7. The best means to get to heaven
10. Merriment (rhymes with girth and begins with M)
11. Singer Jon Bon
17. Sex machine
20. Bugs Bunny for example
22. _____ *Roi*. Alfred Jarry's 1896 surrealist play that forecast the Theatre of the Absurd or dog at the end of situation comedy *Family Ties*: Sit ___, Sit!
24. ___ *You Like It*
25. Extraterrestrial who had to phone home

Solutions to Puzzle on Page 52

TOP TEN PARTY-KILLING SONGS

10. **"MacArthur Park"** by Richard Harris
9. **"Freebird"** by Lynyrd Skynyrd
8. **"Hotel California"** ("No, really, it's a great party. I'm just going for a walk.")

7. **"More Than Words"** (Chick Song by the inappropriately named Extreme)
6. **"Color My World"** (Nice flute solo . . . Not!!)
5. **"Lovin' You"** by Mimi Ripperton
4. **"Billy Don't Be a Hero"**
3. **"From a Distance"** by Bette Midler
2. **Anything by Toto**
1. **Any Disco Tune**

CROSSWORD ANSWERS

A CONVERSATION WITH MADONNA

The other day I called Madonna, you know, just like this, and anyway, I taped the conversation and transcribed it exactly, verbatim, without any embellishment whatsoever:

WAYNE: Hi, Madonna?
MADONNA: Wayne is that you? I was just thinking about you. God, I miss you so much.
WAYNE: Excellent!
MADONNA: I can't wait to see you. I'm in the middle of making a movie and recording a new album and producing a video and planning a tour but I'll drop it all for just a few brief moments with you.
WAYNE: Gee, thanks, Madonna. That's very flattering.
MADONNA: I'm serious, Wayne. I think about you all the time. I can't sleep, I can't eat, I can't work out for two and a half hours a day, I can't maintain a vegetarian diet or anything.
WAYNE: Come on, Madonna. I thought I made myself clear: we're just friends. Can I not call

you up to say hello without you shamelessly throwing yourself at me?

MADONNA: I'm sorry, Wayne. It's just that I love you so much. I can't live without you. You're all I think about. I only go out with other men to try to get you jealous. That's the reason I made *Truth or Dare*. So that there would be all this publicity. I even said "Not!! to Warren a few times to get at you. I only want to be in the public eye so that you'll be forced to see me. It's all a ploy to get your attention. Did you see my "Like a Virgin" video?

WAYNE: Yeah.

MADONNA: I was thinking about you when I made that.

WAYNE: Hang on, that's my call waiting.

MADONNA: I hate call waiting. Come back!

WAYNE: Hello?

GARTH: Hey, Wayne, it's me.

WAYNE: Oh, great, Garth. I've got Madonna on the other line. She's going all mental again.

GARTH: That's so sad. Poor girl.

WAYNE: I know, man. Hang on, I'll be right back.

GARTH: Okay.

WAYNE: Listen, Madonna. I gotta go.

MADONNA: Don't Wayne. Please, stay on a while longer.

WAYNE: No way!

MADONNA: Way! Please, Wayne. I need you.

WAYNE: Sorry, Madonna. You're just going to have to let me go.

MADONNA: (crying) No!!

WAYNE: Bye!

Well, that was my conversation exactly how it happened without any embellishment whatsoever.

(For more information, see page 56.)

MONKEYS MIGHT FLY OUT OF MY BUTT!

I use the expression "and monkeys might fly out of my butt!!" I usually say it when I want to illustrate the implausibility of any given statement. For example a person might say:

PERSON: The Cubs might win the World Series this year.

WAYNE: They might win the World Series . . . Shyeah Rightt!! And monkeys might fly out of my butt!!

How simple. But that led me to thinking: What is the reality of such a statement? What would it actually look like to have monkeys flying out of my butt. Would it be painful? Would the damage to my rectum be irreparable? How would the reverse anal entry affect the winged primates? What were they doing up my butt before they flew out? Were they happy? At the point when they lived in my rectum, were the wings merely vestigial? Were they decorative? Perhaps part of the mating ritual.

So many questions.

For the sake of science, I've made a photographic interpretation of what it would actually look like if monkeys were indeed to fly out of my butt!

(See A Conversation with Madonna, page 53)

OTHER WORLDS

THE PERFECT BABE

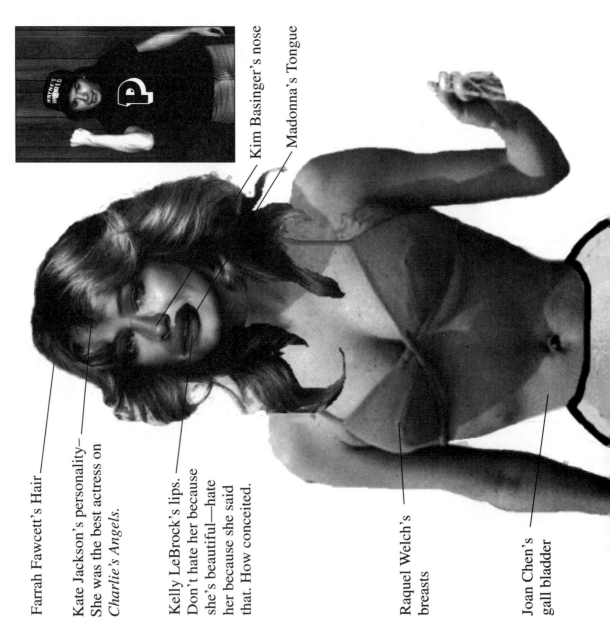

Kim Basinger's nose

Madonna's Tongue

Farrah Fawcett's Hair

Kate Jackson's personality—
She was the best actress on
Charlie's Angels.

Kelly LeBrock's lips.
Don't hate her because
she's beautiful—hate
her because she said
that. How conceited.

Raquel Welch's
breasts

Joan Chen's
gall bladder

Betty Rubble's Ass

Shown here is a composite photograph of the perfect babe using the best of famous babe qualities.

Julia Roberts's legs. Check out those boots she wore in *Pretty Woman* . . . Schwing!!

PHILOSOPHIES

I believe we should all live life like Bugs Bunny. We should have plenty of carrots, a hole in the ground, a mail box with our name written on it, and the freedom to discover our own personal Elmer Fudd. And when we find that Fudd, we should have the freedom to bug the crap out of him.

I believe The Beatles can be imposed on any family dynamic: John is the father, Paul is the mother, and Ringo is the child. Oh, yeah and George, um, ah – he's the quiet one. My philosophy of life can be summed up in four words: Babes, Parties, Brew, and Tunes.

POETRY

Ode to My Guitar

Oh woman of wood and metal
Wailing and bending on tune
of Stairway
Barre chords elude me
They're just too hard
Maybe my hands are just
too small
I don't know, but after I try
doin' them
My wrists are really sore
As if I've got carpel-tunnel
syndrome.
Maybe I should call the Injury
Hot-Line
Evidently, the lawyers don't
charge
Unless they win the case
On second thought
My injuries aren't job related
And so I will suckle from my
guitar teat
Spent
Unloved
Splash

How do Girls Pee?

How do girls pee?
They never showed us
In health class
Splash

Haiku

I hate you haiku
You are too hard
To do
Splash

garth

Typesetter: the poem should
remain in lower case, like
E.E. CUMMINGS.
that one man could love
another man
with the depth
and the breadth
of damon and pythias-like
passion
is my only plea
sweet garth
begrudged
bespectacled
begimped
childlike in beev womb
i know you are
but who am i
splash

Am I a Man?

If I feel pain
Am I a man?
If I appreciate beauty
Am I a man?
If I abhor intolerance
Am I a man?
If I seek harmony
Am I a man?
If I choose to love instead of hate
If I choose to unite instead of
divide
If I choose peace over war
Am I a man?
If I have a vagina and two
lactating breasts
Am I a man?
I guess not
Splash

PSYCHIC PREDICTIONS

I predict that Aerosmith will put out another album.

I predict that there will be a New Year's Rockin' Eve featuring Dick Clark.

I predict that there will be yet another rock 'n' roll charity song.

I predict the Chicago Cubs will not, I repeat not, win the World Series next year.

*I predic*t Jean Dixon will continue to make predictions.

I predict that children will continue to whip snowballs at cars.

I predict there will be a major election in 1992, however, I cannot yet tell at what level of government it will be. I can say this: The winner will be a Democrat (or Republican).

I predict that someone will sue a famous rock star claiming that their song was ripped off.

I predict that Zemtar the Horrible, from the Planet Gremlac, will form a federation of other like-minded class-M planets in order to bypass the planetary mining regulations of the Intergalactic Confederacy in the areas of the Andromeda Galaxy that they currently control. (Unfortunately no one will know that I'm right for another two million years.)

I predict that a formerly famous child star will be in trouble with the law.

QUITE EXCELLENT "WORD TO REPLACE SPHINCTER" CONTEST

When we were thinking about a new word to replace sphincter, we wondered how we would go about it. There were a lot of ideas and someone suggested a contest. We needed something for the letter *Q* so I suggested a Quite Excellent Contest.

Well, the response was overwhelming and it was a tough decision to make but finally we were able to settle on one.

The grand prize winner is Dave McEnroe. Congratulations, Dave. Here goes…

The Quite Excellent New Word is:

RECTUM!!

(rek´•tam) *n.* lower end of the large intestine. *pl.* recta. rectal *a* [L. *rectus*, straight].

Examples:
- You're such a rectum.
- I can't go to gym class today, I'm feeling a bit rectal.
- Wipe that rectal grin off your face.
- You're rectitious.
- You're a rectoid.
- You're a tragic example of rectosity gone unchecked.
- You go off the rect-o-meter.
- I see you dabble in the way of rectery.
- I have seen the rectum and it is you.

Here are some of the quite excellent runner-up contestants and their words:

Linda Carol: *Coccyx*
Stacy Milner: *Shank*
Paul Erikson: *Concubine*
Alison Vickery: *Dollop*
Sada Thompson: *Willie*
Peter Lizard: *Gizzard*
Alice Hind: *Chutney*
Brian Mulroney, Prime Minister of Canada: *Hockey Puck*

Congratulations to you all!

IF I RAN THE NETWORKS

The following is a list of TV shows you could expect to see if I ran the networks:

Metaltainment Tonight
With Mary Hart and Leeza Gibbons.

Hill St. Babes
Chicks in uniforms … Rrrregglle!!

Designing Women—to Look Like Cindy Crawford

Sci-Fi—Excellent!!

The Claudia Schiffer on a Harley Show
A two-hour late night show with just shots of Claudia Schiffer on a Harley Davidson, accompanied by Aerosmith tunes, expressly designed to help you chill out and get over bed spins so you can fall asleep.

Ka-Boom!
A show in which every week, twelve wholesale items are blown up in hyper slow-mo to Pink Floyd tunes.

Babewatch
Exactly what you think it would be.

Chips-22
With Nikki Sixx and Vince Neil from Motley Crüe.

Battlestar Metallica
The future. Planet fights planet. Only this time they have cool haircuts.

Golden Girls—The Babe Years
A half-hour flashback show. Kinda like that beer commercial where all these old ladies fall into the fountain of youth and turn into these amazing babes.

The Pee Wee Herman Show
Hooray for Pee Wee!!!

The Guns 'N' Roses Comedy Hour
A variety show featuring members of Guns 'N' Roses and their wacky and unique brand of humor.

Wayne's World
Excellent! He shoots! He scores!

IF I RAN THE WORLD

I call my show Wayne's World but sometimes I can't help but think, what if it really was Wayne's World? I mean what if I really did run the world?

Well, first I'd make a few changes:

Being a gimp would be a punishable offense.

I would redesign the White House to be made entirely of giant Legos.

I would draft a constitution in which no individual would have the right to hassle another individual (i.e. giving someone an Indian burn, a hurts donut, or a wedgie). The constitution would be founded on the principle of the inalienable right to party.

All people must party!

Women must be free to party!

Young people must party in order that youth need not be wasted on the young.

Old people must party, because partying knows no age limit.

Workers must party! For they have toiled and they have earned it!

And the Amish must party as only the Amish can party, in their own plain way! In short, for each of us to find the party within and to make it a humongoid blowout!

Oh, yeah. And it would be against the law to wear flood pants.

This is what it would look like if you looked Wayne's World up in the encyclopedia:

Amish people partying in their own plain way.

WORLD, WAYNE'S
FACTS IN BRIEF
FORM OF GOVERNMENT: Benevolent Partocracy or The One Humongoid Party System.
CAPITAL: Aurora, Illinois, USA
POPULATION: A Gazillion
MOTTO: Babum, Partium, Tuneum (Babes, Parties, Tunes)
MONEY: The Babe (100 Aerosmiths to one Babe)
NATIONAL ANTHEM: "Stairway to Heaven"
FLAG: A back panel of a Heavy Metal Denim Jacket emblazoned with a picture of Wayne, Heather Locklear, and the word "Aurora" which is in mock Gothic type and surrounded by "zoso symbols" from Led Zeppelin albums.
NATIONAL BIRD: The Chick
CHIEF PRODUCTS: Fun, Allowance, Tunes, Zinc
OFFICIAL LANGUAGE: English and Esperanto (Like love, Esperanto is the international language.)
NATIONAL HOLIDAYS: Aerosmith Day, Zep Day, Locklear Day, Party Day, Partied Out Day (The day after Party Day—no one should do anything. Everyone should just be very still. Music can't be played above four.), Secretary's Day

RECIPE

Here's my recipe for Kraft Macaroni and Cheese with Wieners Cut into It.

Ingredients:
Water
A pot
Wieners
1 box of Kraft Macaroni and Cheese

Directions:
Take a pot and fill it with water. Follow the directions on the back of the Kraft Macaroni and Cheese. While the Kraft Macaroni and Cheese is cooking, take a wiener and cut into slices. Place the wiener slices into the pot containing the Kraft Macaroni and Cheese. When it is all heated, remove from stove. Place in a bowl or a plate (I prefer a plate but a bowl will do just fine) and serve.

HOW TO SCHWING!!

Begin from a standing or seated position. Although me and Garth usually do a "Schwing!!" on a chair or sofa, we will be illustrating a "Schwing!!" from a standing position.

To begin, sit up straight. Let your arms drop to your sides. Just get comfortable. Relax. Take a few deep breaths.

Good.

Now that you're relaxed and comfortable, you'll need to come up with a "Schwing!! Motivator," a comment or phrase which propels you to "Schwing!! into action" so to speak. For demonstration purposes, we'll use the phrase: "Check out Claudia Schiffer's new calendar."

Upon saying the phrase: "Check out Claudia Schiffer's new calendar," I want you to tighten your buttock muscles and tuck in your stomach. (If you should happen to be seated, plant your arms firmly by your sides onto the chair and or sofa and use them to help you pull your torso out of the seat.)

Rotate your pelvis up and out at a ninety-degree angle. Extend your pelvis out as far as it will go while shouting, "Schwing!!" If you can only move a quarter of an inch or so, that's fine. A good rule of thumb is if it hurts, you've extended too far. The adage: "No pain, no gain" is a fallacy. Pain is a signal your body sends to your brain letting you know that something is not right. A "Schwing!!" should be pleasurable and painless. Don't try to show off. The more you practice this the more agile you will become.

When you are through, relax your pelvis and slowly release yourself out of the "Schwing!!" Excellent. You've done it. Give yourself a hand.

You will see that as time goes on, you will get better and better at doing a "Schwing!!" When you feel you are ready you can graduate on to doing multiple "Schwings!!" For example a double "Schwing-Schwing!!" or for those more advanced a triple "Schwing-Schwing-Schwing!!" You can come up with unlimited "Schwing!! Motivators," too. The possibilities are endless. It's all up to you and how much effort you wish to put into it.

* Please note: you should not, I repeat, not, try a "Schwing!!" while sitting on the floor. Doing a "Schwing!!" from the ground can put unnecessary pressure on your lower back.

1

2

SONGS WHERE IT SORTA SOUNDS LIKE THEY'RE SAYING SCHWING!!

"It Don't Mean a Thing if It Ain't Got that Schwing"

"Schwingin' in the Rain" (See Songs Where It Sorta Sounds Like They're Saying Wayne, page 87)

"Schwing Low, Sweet Chariot"

"Schwing, Schwing a Song"

"The Wind Beneath My Schwing"

"Schwing Stairway to Heaven"

SHAMELESS PLUG FOR MY MOVIE

Wayne's World is a comedy about the rock'n'roll misadventures of Wayne Campbell and his sidekick Garth, who host a late-night cable-access show broadcast from their basement in Aurora, Illinois.

Oh, and there's babes in it, too.

Garth and me.

Me with my amazing love interest, Cassandra–schwing!!

Starring: Mike Myers and Dana Carvey
Produced By: Lorne Michaels **Written By:** Mike Myers, Bonnie Turner and Terry Turner **Directed By:** Penelope Spheeris

Coming from Paramount Pictures, Spring 1992

BAD SPELLING IN ROCK

Our nation's youth are constantly being hassled for using bad spelling yet the people who hassle them are always going on and on about the three "R's": Reading, Writing and Arithmetic. Shyeah!! Righttt!! The three "R's"? There's only one "R" and that's Reading. Why didn't they call it the "W.A.R." or the "R.A.W." or the "A.W.R."? How can they sit in judgment? Anyway, here are some examples of bad spelling in rock that we take a lot of heat about:

Ratt (RAT)

The Beatles (BEETLES)

Motley Crüe (CREW)
(There's an umlaut, those two dots, over the "u" in Crüe. That's not even English. That's German!)

Trixter (TRICKSTER)

Tuff (TOUGH)

Enuff Z' Nuff (ENOUGH IS ENOUGH)
(They do the most heinous of all grammatical errors: Cutesy short form. Like Good N' Plenty and referring to midgets as L'il people.)

Def Leppard (DEAF LEOPARD)

Led Zeppelin (LEAD ZEPPELIN)

INXS (IN EXCESS)

Lynyrd Skynyrd (LEONARD SKINNARD)
(author's approximation)

Megadeth (MEGA-DEATH)

Slade (SLAYED)
Who carried the tradition into the songs themselves with "Mama Weer All Crazzee Now," "Cum on Feel the Noise," and "Gudbuy t' Jane."

TOP TEN COOLEST STAR TREKS

TOP TEN COOLEST STAR TREKS PARTY TIME EXCELLENT!

10. The one where Spock hijacks the Enterprise and takes it to Talos IV to save his old captain.

9. The one where Bones surgically alters Kirk to be a Vulcan so he can steal the Klingon's cloaking device.

8. The one where they go back in time to Chicago and dress up as gangsters.

7. The one where the guy who played The Riddler on *Batman* is the half-black/half-white-faced alien; clearly a metaphor for the racial conflicts of its day—Kudos to the late Gene Roddenberry for tackling this issue!

6. The one where Kirk asks the computer an illogical question that causes the computer to explode. (AUTHOR'S NOTE: I think they did that in a whole bunch of episodes.) Kirk asks the computer to define love and then Ka-boom!

5. The one where the whole crew is on the recreation planet and whatever they think about appears. So this Irish guy appears and knocks the crap out of Kirk and keeps saying, "Fight me, Jimmy, fight me, Jimmy." (AUTHOR'S NOTE: Garth and I said "Fight me, Jimmy" to each other for an entire year.)

4. The Ricardo Montalban one they made into a movie.

3. The one where Spock's evil twin has a beard and kills people.

2. The one where Kirk is transferred into a woman's body. If I were a woman for a day, I would have done a lot of different things than Kirk did. Just thinking about it I feel funny. Like when you climb a rope in gym class.

1. The one where they go back in time to depression-era New York City and Kirk has to let Joan Collins die even though he's in love with her so history won't be changed and Spock has to wear a stupid wool cap like a gimp so they can't see his ears.

STUPID QUESTIONS

These are questions that have been plaguing me for years. I've kept a journal.
Here they are.

In England do they call ZZ Top Zed Zed Top?

Why do all head shops smell the same?

Why do all head shops have posters with monkeys sitting on the toilet?

Why do people think that's funny?

What is Fahrvergnügen?

Why do Roadies carry so many keys?

Why do Roadies always say, "Check one, Check two, Sibilance, Sibilance"?

Why do people go "Woo!" when the lights go down at a concert?

Why does every culture in the world have their own equivalent of Mommy, Mommy Jokes?

If God is supposed to be all-loving, then why is there so much suffering in the world?

Why were there two Darren Stevens in Bewitched?

Why did Barney Rubble have two different voices?

Why do some people get teary-eyed talking about Jim Morrison when they've never listened to a Doors album in their life?

Why do people take those chemical glow sticks to concerts?

What do they do with them once the concert is over?

AEROSMITH TRANSCRIPT

Garth's cousin Barry is a roadie for Aerosmith. Roadies are the bottom feeders in the great babe food chain. Anyway, that's how we got the greatest band in the world on my show. The only thing is I had to have Barry on as a guest.

Okay, so Garth and I met Steven Tyler, Joe Perry, Brad Whitford, Tom Hamilton and Joey Kramer. Aerosmith was sitting in my breakfast nook where I eat my Nut & Honey every morning. The bogus part is that my mom showed Aerosmith my hospital pictures from when I had meningitis and took them on a tour of the house. It was very embarrassing.

But once the "Oh Mighty Ones" were in the basement everything was cool. We told a lot of people that they might be on the show and a lot of people had a lot of questions. Here's a transcript of that segment.

WAYNE: Is it true you guys don't do drugs or alcohol anymore?

JOE PERRY: Yeah that's right. No drugs. No alcohol. We've never felt better.

WAYNE: No way.

JOE PERRY: Way.

WAYNE: No Way!

JOE PERRY: Way!

WAYNE: Okay. Next question, Garth.

GARTH: This question is for Steven. Are those really your lips or are they lip implants like Barbara Hershey had in the movie *Beaches*?

STEVEN TYLER: These lips are mine.

GARTH: Excellent.

WAYNE: With the recent developments in Eastern Europe, do you think that

Communism is on the decline or is this just a temporary setback?

STEVEN TYLER: Wow, man, that's a hard question. But I would have to respond with a qualified yes. Although it seems that socialism is in repose, until you remove the Stalinist era Party apparatchiks there will be no real change in the Soviet Union.

TOM HAMILTON: I disagree. There's never been a blueprint for a proletarian dictatorship so it's bound to make mistakes. But if you study history you'll see that since the rise of the nation-state socialism has been an historical inevitability, dude.

It had always been my fantasy to play with those guys and believe it or nay, I did (See Lyrics, page 85).

For further transcripts send $2.00 to Journal Graphics.

AUTHOR'S NOTE:

At the time of this conversation, Tom Hamilton had no idea of what was to transpire in the mighty Soviet Empire; that forces of democracy and dissent within that beleaguered Socialist union would rise up and bring the so-called "proletarian dictatorship" to its knees. Tom felt, with his comment that there was no blueprint for a socialist state, that the historical inevitability of dialectical materialism was more durable.

Steven Tyler, however, correctly sensed that the problem was with the apparatchiks, though it should be noted that he was unwilling to predict when their reign would ultimately end.

Cool, huh?

THINGS THAT MAKE YOU GO HMMM

C+C Music Factory have a song called "Things That Make You Go Hmmm." We'd like to add to that list.

- Having a frog in your throat and trying to clear it.

- Being bound and gagged and poked at with a very sharp pin. You try to scream and all that comes out is "Hmmm."

- Being hit on the head with a brick and temporarily losing your ability to speak. As you go through speech therapy to relearn the vowel sounds, all you're able to do initially is go "Hmmm."

- Eating a huge bowl of pasta and having someone ask if it tastes good while you're mid-bite and all you're able to say is "Hmmm."

- Having someone put a gun to your head and demand you go "Hmmm."

ELLENT

UNECESSARY ZOOM

INSTRUCTIONS: *Hold book open with photo facing you in hands and extend arms. Bend arms and bring book in close to your eyes and then extend out once again. Continue bending and flexing arms while screaming "WHOA!! and WAAAAAAAAAA!!!!" alternately.*

URBAN MYTHS

These are stories of actual people. Not anybody I know firsthand, but friends of friends. It's true. I swear.

1. This girl was babysitting and got drunk. She took the dog for a walk during a rainstorm and when she came home she dried the dog off by putting it in the microwave oven and the dog exploded.

2. This girl was babysitting Mikey from LIFE cereal and he ate pop rocks and then drank soda causing his head to explode while in her care.

3. This girl was babysitting and she got a bump on her face which she thought was a zit. She put zit medicine on it and it wouldn't go away. Eventually she went to the doctor who told her it was a spider bite and then she was sleeping and she felt a tickling on her face and she ran to the mirror and it turned out that the bump was a nest of baby spiders and they just had hatched on her face.

4. This girl was babysitting and there was this forest fire and it was threatening this guy's log cabin so he was evacuated. When he came back home he was happy to see that his house was still standing. Only the trees on his property had burnt down. But the guy discovered that in one of the burnt trees was a dead guy in scuba gear. What he later found out was that this guy had been scuba diving when one of those forest fire airplanes that skims water from lakes had sucked him into the water tank and dowsed him onto the fire.

5. This girl was babysitting except for this one night and the couple she baby-sits for went out for the evening and took their baby with them and came home to find that their house had been robbed. The only items that the burglar left was their camera and their toothbrushes. They continued to use their toothbrushes and finished the roll of film on the camera. A few weeks later the couple went to develop the film that was in the camera and in it there were pictures of the burglar, sticking the couple's toothbrushes up his butt.

6. This girl was babysitting and one day she exploded.

OUT ON VIDEO

WAYNE AND GARTH
OUT ON VIDEO
PARTY TIME
EXCELLENT!

The following is Mine and Garth's review of stuff out on video:

Freddy's Dead—The Final Nightmare
WAYNE: I liked it.
GARTH: I liked it, too.

Thelma & Louise
WAYNE: The moral of the movie: Men bad—Women good. I thought it sucked.
GARTH: Yeah, It sucked.
WAYNE: It was a chick movie.

Dying Young
Starring that Babe, Julia Roberts (Rrrregglle)
WAYNE: Didn't see it.
GARTH: Didn't see it.

Bingo
Starring . . . Some Dog?
WAYNE: SUCKED.
GARTH: Sucked.
WAYNE: Sucked donkeys.

Robin Hood: Prince of Thieves
WAYNE: Shyeahhh!! Rightttt!!
GARTH: As if!

Regarding Henry
GARTH: It sucked big time.
WAYNE: I kinda liked it …NOT!!

Europa, Europa
WAYNE: Directed by Agnieszka Holland, this film is a comic epic of survival dealing with conformity and brutality in war torn Europe. Reminiscent of Voltaire's *Candide*, it lacks the sanctimonious cynicism of most Franco-German productions.
GARTH: Sucked!

Terminator 2
Starring Linda Hamilton—Manly, yes,
but I like her too.

WAYNE: Excellent. He shoots, He scores.
GARTH: Mega-Excellent.

We've provided a handy "quick reference" guide for your perusal:

MOVIE	WAYNE	GARTH
FREDDY'S DEAD—THE FINAL NIGHTMARE	LIKE	LIKE
THELMA & LOUSE	SUCKED (CHICK MOVIE)	SUCKED
DYING YOUNG	DIDN'T SEE	DIDN'T SEE
BINGO	SUCKED DONKEYS	SUCKED
ROBIN HOOD: PRINCE OF THIEVES	SHYEAHH RIGHTTT	AS IF
REGARDING HENRY	KINDA LIKED IT…NOT!	SUCKED BIG TIME
EUROPA, EUROPA	FRANCO-GERMAN PRODUCTION	SUCKED
TERMINATOR 2	EXCELLENT. HE SHOOTS, HE SCORES	MEGA-EXCELLENT

TOP TEN VIDEO BABES

TOP TEN *VIDEO BABES* *PARTY TIME* *EXCELLENT!*

10. **"1999"** by Prince: The lingerie-wearing keyboard player.

9. **"Simply Irresistible"** by Robert Palmer: The babe in the bottom left corner.

8. **"I Touch Myself"** by The Divinyls: The masked babe.

7. **"Love in an Elevator"** by Aerosmith: The brunette mannequin babe.

6. **"Hot for Teacher"** by Van Halen: The teacher babe.

5. **"Legs"** by ZZ Top: The pouty blonde babe.

4. **"Simply Irresistible"** by Robert Palmer: The third babe from the left. Top row.

3. **"Freedom"** by George Michael: The dancing-around-with-headphones-on babe.

2. **"Rock the Cradle of Love"** by Billy Idol: The neighbor babe.

1. **"Cherry Pie"** by Warrant: The rollerskating babe.

VIEWER MAIL

Dear Wayne & Garth:

   I'm writing to you from a jail somewhere in Montana. I hope this letter gets to you. If it does it will be a minor miracle. I managed to slip this letter to a Red Cross official when he came and visited me in my cell. You see, I'm a member of the Kiss Army. I was drafted in 1975; outfitted in Kiss regalia; issued my Kiss German Army Helmet and was assigned to the Peter Criss "CAT" brigade. I went on a tour of duty following Kiss in the Great Lakes area. And then in 1976 I was captured and taken prisoner by the enemy. Although the conditions are harsh, we are allowed to watch episodes of "Wayne's World." I was wondering if you could send me an autographed photo of yourself.

Sincerely,
Jeff Josephson

   P.S. We're planning a breakout tomorrow. I've rigged up this hot air balloon device. I've never written a fan letter before and I feel a bit squishy.

Dear Jeff:

   To say that you are mental would be an understatement. Besides the fact that you are not being held captive by any vague so-called "enemy," the fascistic Nazi overtones of the Kiss Army featuring it's slashed-"S" logo make it clear that you are Cuckoo for Cocoa Puffs.

Party On,
Wayne Campbell & Garth Algar

   P.S. Enclosed please find the autographed photo you requested.

Dear Wayne & Garth:

I'm a manager of a national fast food chicken restaurant chain that was started in Kentucky by an elderly man with a goatee and a confederate army record (sorry for being so vague, but I worked hard to get where I am and I don't want to put my job in jeopardy).

Anyway, one night, just as I was closing up, this mean-looking guy came into my restaurant. Boy, was he huge. Let's just say this: his muscles had muscles. His thighs were bigger than my whole body (if you know what I mean … Let me put it this way—although we sell chicken thighs, the thighs I'm referring to weren't those of a chicken, if you know what I mean).

So, it was clear that he wanted something other than chicken. (If you know what I mean—and I don't mean fries, biscuits, corn on the cob or soda if you know what I mean).

He pulls out a gun and, as I'm getting out money from the register, the whole time my mind wanders to thoughts other than chicken (If you know what I mean—I'm of course referring to getting help and I don't mean help between two chickens).

I hand him the money and he grabs me by the throat and says that if I call the cops he'll come back and break my neck. (He meant my actual neck, of course—not a chicken neck. If you know what I mean.)

Anyway, he took the money and left and I never called the police. Do you think I was wrong?

Sincerely,
Name and address withheld upon request.

P.S. Would you please send me an autographed photo of you guys. My name is Ryan Lane. I live at 1221 Mill Way.

Dear Name and address withheld upon request:

It really is not our place to judge what you did. You and only you must decide whether or not you made the right decision. (If you know what we mean. And we don't mean chicken decision.)

Party on,
Wayne Campbell and Garth Algar

P.S. Enclosed please find the autographed picture you requested.

Dear Wayne:

What do you do if some incredible chick is talking to you and every time she talks to you you think you're gonna hurl?

Sincerely,
Stephen Milmoe

Dear Stephen:

I say hurl. If you blow chunks and she comes back, she's yours. If you spew and she bolts, it was never meant to be.

Party On,
Wayne Campbell

P.S. Enclosed please find an autographed photo.

FAVORITE WAR NAME OF ALL TIME

THE PUNIC WARS: FIRST AND SECOND

What makes it interesting is that there are no people called Punics and there is no Punicia. It was a series of wars between the Romans and the Carthaginians, led by General Hannibal. The highlight was the use of elephants by the Carthaginians over the Alps to temporarily defeat the Romans.

Of course, my favorite part of the Punic Wars is that the word Punic sounds dirty.

See Shameless Filler, page 32

HOW TO SING THE WAYNE'S WORLD THEME

This is the long-version theme song that I sang with Aerosmith. It's available on the Aerosmith maxi-single for the song "The Other Side" on Geffen Records.

IT'S WAYNE'S WORLD
IT'S WAYNE'S WORLD
IT'S PARTY TIME
IT'S EXCELLENT
IT'S WAYNE'S WORLD
IT'S WAYNE'S WORLD
IT'S PARTY TIME
IT'S EXCELLENT
CHICKS GO MENTAL
WHEN WE GO DOWN THE STREET
IT'S WAYNE & GARTH
THAT THEY WANT TO MEET
WE'RE DOWN IN THE BASEMENT
PLAYING WITH OUR TOYS
AND IF YOU DO NOT LIKE IT
YOU'RE A SPHINCTER BOY
IT'S WAYNE'S WORLD
IT'S WAYNE'S WORLD
IT'S PARTY TIME
IT'S EXCELLENT

FAMOUS WAYNES OF ALL TIME

FAMOUS WAYNES OF ALL TIME   PARTY TIME   EXCELLENT!

Wayne Gretzky—The Great One

Wayne Newton—Danka Shane

John Wayne—The Duke

Wayne Dyer—Author of many useful self-help books

Bruce Wayne—A.k.a. Batman. Excellent!

Keenan Ivory Wayne—An excellent comedic actor

Wayne Rogers—Trapper John, M.D.

Wayne Ona Ryder—The babalicious movie star

Claude Waynes—The very famous actor

Wayne George Washington—The father of our country

SONGS WHERE IT SORTA SOUNDS LIKE THEY'RE SAYING WAYNE

"Up Up and a Wayne"

"Here Comes the Wayne Again"

"Penny Wayne"

"Blame It on the Wayne"

"Singin' in the Wayne"

"Do You Know the Wayne to San Jose?"

"I Did It My Wayne"

"Waynedrops Keep Fallin' on My Head"

"Wayne Stairway to Heaven"

WAYNE'S WORK OUT:

"Air" bench press   **1**

2

Eddie arm stretches (remember to make a Van Halen half smile/ half grimace)

Lifting the amp

Foot on monitor leg stretches

SWEATIN' TO THE METAL

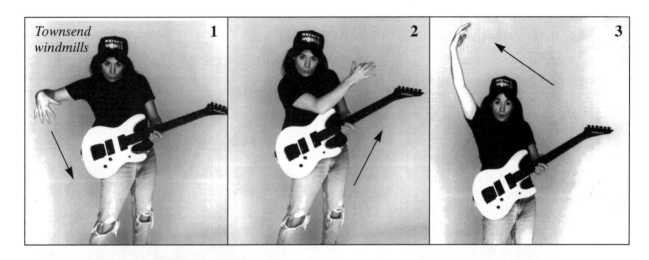

Townsend windmills — 1, 2, 3

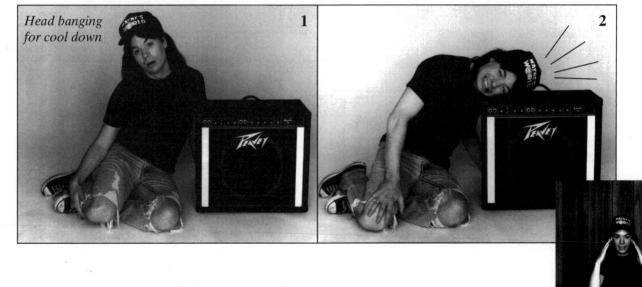

Head banging for cool down — 1, 2

WHERE'S WAYNE?

And where's Mike Myers; Todd Rundgren; Alannah Myles; Lara Flynn Boyle; Ed O'Neal; Brian Doyle Murray; Bruno Kirby; George Wendt; Michael Jordan; Martha Quinn; Peter Falk; Elvira; Jeff Daniels; Timothy Leary; Laraine Newman; Color Me Bad and Garth?

XAVIAR CUGAT & CHARO: WHAT WENT WRONG?

Okay, so I needed to get a subject beginning with the letter *X* for my book so I called up Charo, "The Coochi Coochi Girl," at her house in Hawaii and asked her a few questions about her ex-husband, Xaviar Cugat. Here's how the conversation went:

WAYNE: Hi, Charo?
CHARO: Hi, is this Wayne?
WAYNE: Yeah. How's it going?
CHARO: Pretty good.
WAYNE: What's Hawaii like? It looks really cool.
CHARO: It's very nice. The weather is lovely all year round and we have the most exquisite sunsets.
WAYNE: Excellent. Oh, hang on a second, that's my call waiting.
CHARO Okay.
WAYNE: Hello?
GARTH: Hey, Wayne.
WAYNE: Garth, I'm on the phone with Charo–long distance.

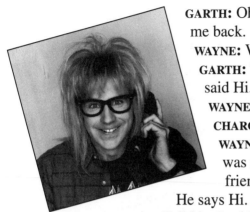

GARTH: Oh, cool. Call me back.

WAYNE: Will do.

GARTH: Tell her I said Hi.

WAYNE: Charo?

CHARO: Yes?

WAYNE: That was my best friend Garth. He says Hi.

CHARO: Tell him I said Hi back.

WAYNE: Will do. So you were married to Xaviar Cugat, right?

CHARO: Yes.

WAYNE: That's why I'm calling. I need to know: What went wrong?

CHARO: Well, Wayne, it's one of those things. Cugy was much older than me and, like a lot of people in relationships, you begin to grow apart. I guess that's what happened to us.

WAYNE: Interesting. Well, thanks, Charo.

CHARO: You're welcome, Wayne.

WAYNE: Oh, wait, one more question. Did you ever notice that *Green Acres*, *Petticoat Junction*, and *The Beverly Hillbillies* were all linked in the same reality?

CHARO: Well, I'm not exactly sure what you mean.

WAYNE: Oh, just that Jethro would appear on *Petticoat Junction* and Sam Drucker could be seen sometimes on *The Beverly Hillbillies*.

CHARO: Yeah, I never really looked at it that way but now that you mention it, I remember Arnold Ziffle once visited the Clampett Mansion.

WAYNE: Good call. Well, I should go now. Thanks a lot.

CHARO: You're welcome. Bye-bye.

WAYNE: Good-bye.

TOP TEN SONGS TO GET YOU PSYCHED

TOP TEN WAYNE'S WORLD PARTY TIME EXCELLENT!

10. **"Happy"** by The Rolling Stones

9. **"You Shook Me All Night Long"** by ACDC

8. **"School's Out"** by Alice Cooper

7. **"Sharp-Dressed Man"** by ZZ Top

6. **"Pictures of Lily"** by The Who

5. **"Bat Out of Hell"** by Meatloaf

4. **"Ballroom Blitz"** by Sweet

3. **"Rock 'n' Roll"** by Led Zeppelin

2. **"Dream On"** by Aerosmith

1. **"Under Pressure"** by David Bowie and Queen

ZEEK ZANZIBAR- UP CLOSE AND PERSONAL

I needed something for the letter Z so I looked in the phone book and I found this guy named Zeek Zanzibar. Way!! So anyway I called him up and here's what he had to say.

WAYNE: Hello? Is Zeek Zanzibar there?

ZEEK: Speaking.

WAYNE: Hi, my name is Wayne Campbell.

ZEEK: What do you want?

WAYNE: I'm writing a book in an A to Z format and I needed to write something for the letter Z. So I looked up Z in the phone book and found your name … Oh, I'm sorry, that's my call waiting. Can you hang on a second?

ZEEK: Sure.

WAYNE: Hello?

GARTH: Hey, Wayne.

WAYNE: Garth, you have the uncanny ability to call me when I'm on the other line.

GARTH: Gee, thanks.

WAYNE: I'll call you right back.

GARTH: Okay.

WAYNE: Hello, Zeek?

ZEEK: Yep.

WAYNE: Sorry. So anyway, I just want to talk to you and transcribe the conversation. Do you have a few minutes to talk?

ZEEK: Well, actually I was just heading out to get my allergy shots.

WAYNE: Oh, yeah? What are you allergic to?

ZEEK: Pollen, mold, and shrimp.

WAYNE: Bummer.

ZEEK: Yeah. Well, I should go.

WAYNE: Okay. I guess I have enough for my book. I'm just curious though. Is your real name Zeek Zanzibar?

ZEEK: Uh, huh.

WAYNE: Cool. Thanks a lot.

ZEEK: No problem. Good luck with your book.

WAYNE: Thanks.

ZEEK: Bye.

WAYNE: Good-bye.

Well, that's all the time I have for my book, until my next book. Good night and Party On!